DETAIL

OF THE

SETS OF HARNESS

REQUIRED FOR THE

VARIOUS NATURES OF SERVICE PATTERN VEHICLES.

FireStep Publishing
Gemini House
136-140 Old Shoreham Road
Brighton
BN3 7BD

www.firesteppublishing.com

First published by the General Staff, War Office 1915.
First published in this format by FireStep Editions,
an imprint of FireStep Publishing, in association with
the National Army Museum, 2013.

www.nam.ac.uk

ISBN 978-1-908487-72-8

Cover design FireStep Publishing
Typeset by FireStep Publishing
Printed and bound in Great Britain

Please note: *In producing in facsimile from original historical documents, any
imperfections may be reproduced and the quality may be lower than modern
typesetting or cartographic standards.*

DETAIL

OF THE

SETS OF HARNESS

REQUIRED FOR THE

VARIOUS NATURES OF
SERVICE PATTERN VEHICLES.

LONDON:

PRINTED FOR HIS MAJESTY'S STATIONERY OFFICE,
BY HARRISON & SONS, ST. MARTIN'S LANE, W.C.

PRINTERS IN ORDINARY TO HIS MAJESTY.

1915.

FiReStep
Editions

These Tables have been drawn up for the guidance of all concerned, to shew the sets of harness required for the various descriptions of service pattern vehicles.

They must not be quoted as an authority for demanding harness from the Army Ordnance Department.

HARNESS FOR VEHICLES FITTED WITH POLE-BARS, EXCEPT THOSE OF SIEGE AND HEAVY ARTILLERY.

Description.	Wheel. Number per double set.	Lead. Number per double set.	Remarks.
SECTION No. 2.			
Ropes, head, hemp, with ring	2	2	
SECTION No. 5.			*R.H.A. only.
Harness, pole draught, G.S.:—			
Breechings	2	—	
Collars, breast	2	2	†"Wire, long," can
Leggings, drivers	1	1	be used in lieu,
Neck-pieces, pole-bar	2	—	except for R.E.
Pads, collar	2	2	tool carts.
* „ luggage, R.H.A. (with surcingle)	1	1	
*Pannels. luggage pad, R.H.A. pairs	1	1	‡Not used with pole
Straps, collar pad ... ... „	2	2	bar vehicles but
„ hip, long, wheel ... „	2	—	carried in vehicle
„ loin, lead	—	2	for use if required
„ neck	2	2	to hook into a
†Traces, wire, adjustable ... pairs	2	—	vehicle with pole
„ „ long ... ... „	—	2	chains.
„ „ short ... ... „	—	2	
‡Tugs, neck-piece	2	—	§The number must
Whips, drivers	1	1	be doubled when
			saddles are issued
SECTION No. 6.			for " off " horses,
Saddlery, universal :—			viz., in R.F.A.
Bits, portmouth, reversible	2	2	and R.E. technical
Heads, bridle...	2	2	vehicles.
§Blankets, saddle	1	1	
‖Collars, head	2	2	‖" Small," " large,"
§Girths, leather, pattern '84	1	1	" extra large," as
§Leathers, stirrup	2	2	required.
§Pannels. numnah ... ... pairs	1	1	
¶Reins, bit	2	2	¶" Reins, bearing,"
§Saddles, S.A.	1	1	for " off " horses
§Stirrups	2	2	can be used in
§Straps, baggage	3	3	lieu.
§Surcingles, leather	1	1	

The following extending straps should be demanded where necessary for fitting harness to heavy draught horses :—

Breechings, straps, extending...	For extending breechings one is used at each end of breeching ; also for extending neck-piece pole-bar one or more as necessary.
Surcingle, straps, extending ...	For extending surcingle, neck straps and straps hip, long, wheel, as necessary.
Girths, pieces, extending ...	For extending girths.

(B 3685)   Wt. w. 1380—1214   10M   5/15   H & S   P. 15/266

HARNESS FOR VEHICLES FITTED WITH POLE-CHAINS
(INSTEAD OF POLE-BARS) SUCH AS WAGONS G.S., &c.

BREAST COLLAR, DRAUGHT.

Description.	Wheel. Number per double set.	Remarks.
SECTION No. 2.		
Ropes, head, hemp, with ring	2	
SECTION No. 5.		
Harness, pole draught, G.S. :—		
Breechings, large...	2	
Collars, breast	2	
Leggings, drivers	1	
Neckpieces, pole-bar	2	
Pads, collar, extra large	2	
Straps, collar pad ... ... pairs	2	
„ hip, long, wheel ... ... „	2	
„ neck	2	
*Traces, wire, adjustable ... pairs	2	*" Wire long " can be
Tugs, neck-piece	2	used in lieu.
Whips, drivers	1	
SECTION No. 6.		
Saddlery, universal :—		
Blankets, saddle	1	
Bits, portmouth, reversible :—		
Heads, bridle, extra large	2	
Collars, head, extra large	2	
Girths, leather, pattern '84	1	
Leathers, stirrup	2	
Pannels, numnah ... ... pairs	1	†" Reins bearing " for
†Reins, bit	2	"off" horses can be
Saddle, S.A.	1	used in lieu.
Stirrups	2	
Straps, baggage	3	‡ Or bits, portmouth,
Surcingles, leather	1	reversible, large
Miscellaneous articles:—		when considered
‡Bits, snaffle, van	2	necessary.

The following extending straps should be demanded where necessary for fitting harness to heavy draught horses :—

Breechings, straps, extending ... For extending breechings, one is used at each end of breeching ; also for extending neck-piece pole-bar, one or more as necessary.

Surcingle, straps, extending ... For extending surcingles, neck straps and straps, hip, long, wheel, as necessary.

Girths, pieces, extending... ... For extending girths.

Note.—For long rein driving, the following articles are also required :—

Reins, driving, long ... ... sets	1
„ „ pieces extending	1
Whips, driving, Mark III	1
Rings, rein, driving	4

NECK COLLAR, DRAUGHT.

Description.	Wheel. Number per double set.	Remarks.
SECTION No. 2.		
Ropes, head, hemp, with ring	2	
SECTION No. 5.		
Harness, pole draught, G.S :—		
Breechings, large	2	
*Chains, hame, with ring...	2	* To connect hames
Collars, neck, large	2	at bottom.
Hames, with rings ... ... pairs	2	
Leggings, drivers	1	
Pads, collar, extra large	2	
†Pieces, buckling, 1 inch	2	† To connect with
Straps, collar pad ... ... pairs	2	wither strap.
,, hame, 42 inches	2	
,, hip, long, wheel ... ... pairs	2	‡ To connect front
,, wither, 1 in. × 18 ins.	2	of traces with hames.
‡Traces, chain, hame attachment pairs	2	
§ ,, wire, adjustable ... ,,	2	§ " Wire, long," can
Whips, drivers	1	be used in lieu.
SECTION No. 6.		
Saddlery, universal :—		
Blankets, saddle	1	
Bits, portmouth, reversible :—		
Heads, bridle, extra large	2	
Collars, head, extra large	2	
Girths, leather, pattern '84	1	
Leathers, stirrup	2	
Pannels, numnah ... ... pairs	1	‖ " Reins, bearing,"
‖Reins, bit	2	for " off " horses can
Saddle, S.A.	1	be used in lieu.
Stirrups	2	
Straps, baggage	3	¶ Or bits, port-
Surcingles, leather	1	mouth, reversible,
Miscellaneous articles :		large, when con-
¶Bits, snaffle, van	2	siderd necessary.

The following extending straps should be demanded where necessary for
fitting harness to heavy draught horses :—

Breechings, straps, extending ... For extending breechings, one is
used at each end of breeching ; also
for extending neck-piece pole-bar,
one or more as necessary.

Surcingle straps, extending ... For extending surcingles, neck
straps and straps, hip, long, wheel,
as necessary.

Girths, pieces, extending ... ... For extending girths.

Note.—For long rein driving the following articles are also required :—

Reins, driving, long ... ... sets 1
,, ,, pieces, extending 1
Whips, driving, Mark III 1

HARNESS "EMERGENCY" PATTERN ISSUABLE IN PAIR HORSE
G.S. WAGONS IN LIEU OF HARNESS, POLE DRAUGHT, G.S.

Description.	Wheel. Number per double set.	Remarks.
SECTION No. 2.		
Ropes, head, hemp, with ring	2	
SECTION No. 5.		
Harness, pole draught, G.S. :—		
*Chains, hame, with ring	2	* To connect hames
·Collars, neck, large	2	at bottom.
Hames, with rings ... ... pairs	2	
Pads, collar	2	
Reins, driving, long, special ... sets	1	
Straps, collar, pad ... ... pairs	2	
„ hame	2	
Traces, "emergency" pattern ... pairs	2	
Whips, driving, Mark III	1	
SECTION No. 6.		
Saddlery, universal:—		
†Bits, portmouth, reversible	2	† Or bits, snaffle, van,
Heads, bridle	2	when considered
Collars, head	2	necessary.

HARNESS FOR SHAFT DRAUGHT VEHICLES, EXCEPT GUN-CARRIAGES OF SIEGE ARTILLERY.

(If only One Horse is to be used, the "Off" Set is Requisite.)

BREAST COLLAR DRAUGHT.

Description.	Number per single "off" wheel set.	Number per single " near " wheel set.	Remarks.
SECTION No. 2.			
Ropes, head, hemp, with ring ...	1	1	
SECTION No. 5.			
Harness, pole draught, G.S.:—			
Breechings	1	1	
Collars, breast	1	1	
Leggings, drivers	—	1	
Pads, collar	1	1	
Straps, collar pad ... ... pairs	1	1	
,, hip, long, wheel... ,,	1	1	
,, neck	1	1	
*Traces, wire, adjustable pairs	1	1	* " Wire, long," can be used in lieu.
Whips, drivers	—	1	
Harness, shaft draught:—			
Bands, back	1	—	
Girths, luggage	1	—	
Numnahs, felt, luggage	1	—	
Pannels, numnah, luggage pairs	1	—	
Reins, side	1	—	
Saddles, luggage, I.A., large ...	1	—	
Straps, girth	4	—	
Tugs, back-band	2	—	
SECTION No. 6.			
Saddlery, universal :—			
Bits, portmouth, reversible ...	1	1	
Heads, bridle, large	1	1	
Blankets, saddle	—	1	
Collars, head, large	1	1	
Girths, leather, pattern '84 ...	—	1	
Leathers, stirrup...	—	2	
Pannels, numnah... ... pairs	—	1	
†Reins, bit	1	1	† " Reins, bearing," for " off " horse can be used in lieu.
Saddles, S.A.	—	1	
Stirrups	—	2	
Straps, baggage	3	3	
Surcingles, leather	1	1	

HARNESS FOR SHAFT DRAUGHT VEHICLES, EXCEPT GUN-CARRIAGES OF SIEGE ARTILLERY.

(IF ONLY ONE HORSE IS TO BE USED, THE "OFF" SET IS REQUISITE.)

NECK COLLAR DRAUGHT.

Description.	Number per single "off" wheel set.	Number per single "near" wheel set.	Remarks.
SECTION No. 2.			
Ropes, head, hemp, with ring	1	1	
SECTION No. 5.			
Harness, pole draught, G.S. :—			
Breechings	1	1	
Chains, hame, with ring	1	1	
Collars, neck	1	1	
Hames, with rings ... ... pairs	1	1	
Leggings, drivers	—	1	
Pads, collar	1	1	
Straps, collar pad ... ... pairs	1	1	
" hip, long, wheel ... "	1	1	
" hame	1	1	
Traces, chain, hame attachment pairs	1	1	
* " wire, adjustable ... "	1	1	* "Wire long" can
Whips, drivers	—	1	be used in lieu.
Harness, shaft draught :—			
Bands, back	1	—	
Girths, luggage...	1	—	
Numnahs, felt, luggage	1	—	
Pannels, numnah, luggage ... pairs	1	—	
Reins, side	1	—	
Saddles, luggage, I.A., large... ...	1	—	
Straps, girth	4	—	
Tugs, back-band	2	—	
Saddlery, universal :—			
Bits, portmouth, reversible	1	1	
Heads, bridle, large...	1	1	
Blankets, saddle	—	1	
Collars, head, large	1	1	
Girths, leather, pattern '84	—	1	
Leathers, stirrup	—	2	
Pannels, numnah ... ... pairs	—	1	
†Reins, bit	1	1	† "Reins bearing"
Saddles, S.A.	—	1	for "off" horse
Stirrups	—	2	can be used in
Straps, baggage	3	3	lieu.
Surcingles, leather	1	1	

HARNESS FOR VEHICLES FITTED FOR POLE DRAUGHT (WITH POLE-BARS) OF HEAVY AND SIEGE ARTILLERY ONLY.

Description.	Wheel. Number per double set.	Lead. Number per double set.	Remarks.
SECTION No. 2.			
Ropes, head, hemp, with ring	2	2	
SECTION No. 5.			
Harness, pole draught, G.S.:—			
Breechings, large	2	—	
Collars, breast	2	2	
Leggings, drivers	1	1	*" Wire, long " can
Neck-pieces, pole-bar	2	—	be used in lieu.
Pads, collar, large	2	2	
Straps, collar pad ... ... pairs	2	2	
,, hip, long, wheel ... ,,	2	—	† In addition to
,, loin, lead	—	2	" adjustable " or
,, neck	2	2	" wire, long."
*Traces, wire, adjustable ... pairs	2	—	
,, ,, long ... ,,	—	2	‡Not used with pole-
,, ,, short ... ... ,,	—	2	bar but carried in
† ,, ,, wheel ... ... ,,	2	—	vehicle for use if
‡Tugs, neck-piece	2	—	required to hook
Whips, drivers	1	1	into a vehicle with pole chains.
SECTION No. 6.			
Saddlery, universal:—			
Bits, portmouth, reversible, large ...	2	2	§The number must
Heads bridle, extra large	2	2	be doubled when
§Blankets, saddle	1	1	saddles are issued
‖Collars, head, extra large	2	2	for " off " horses.
§Girths. leather, pattern '84	1	1	
§Leathers, stirrup	2	2	‖Or"special large."
§Pannels, numnah ... ... pairs	1	1	
¶Reins, bit	2	2	¶"Reins, bearing,"
§Saddle, S.A.	1	1	for " off " horses
§Stirrups	2	2	can be used in
§Straps, baggage	3	3	lieu.
§Surcingles, leather	1	1	

The following extending straps should be demanded where necessary for fitting harness to heavy draught horses :—

Breechings, straps, extending... For extending breechings one is used at each end of breeching ; also for extending neck-piece pole-bar one or more as necessary.

Surcingles, straps, extending... For extending surcingles, neck straps and straps. hip, long, wheel, as necessary.

Girths, pieces, extending ... For extending girths.

HARNESS FOR SIEGE ARTILLERY GUN-CARRIAGES FITTED FOR SHAFT DRAUGHT.

(IF THERE ARE TWO PAIRS OF SHAFTS FOR FOUR-A-BREAST DRAUGHT, THE FRAME PAIR OF SHAFTS SHOULD BE REMOVED. SWINGLETREES WITH QUICK RELEASE FITTINGS ARE REQUISITE, OR THE FITTINGS FOR TRACES ON THE SPLINTER BAR REQUIRE ALTERATION AS DIRECTED IN PARAGRAPH 16,525, LIST OF CHANGES IN WAR MATERIEL, IF SUCH HAS NOT ALREADY BEEN DONE.)

Description.	Wheel. Number per double set.	Lead. Number per double set.	Remarks.
SECTION No. 2.			
Ropes, head, hemp, with ring	2	2	
SECTION No. 5.			
Harness, pole draught, G.S.:—			
Breechings, large...	2	—	
Collars, breast	2	2	
Leggings, drivers	1	1	
Pads, collar, large	2	2	
Straps, collar pad... ... ... pairs	2	2	
,, hip, long, wheel ... ... ,,	2	—	
,, loin, lead	—	2	
,, neck	2	2	
*Traces, wire, adjustable... ... pairs	2	—	* " Wire, long," can be used in lieu.
,, ,, long ... ... ,,	—	2	
,, ,, short ... ... ,,	—	2	
† ,, ,, wheel ... ... ,,	2	—	† In addition to "adjustable," or "wire, long."
Harness, shaft draught:—			
Girths, luggage	1	—	
Numnahs, felt, luggage	1	—	
Pannels, numnah, luggage ... pairs	1	—	
Reins, side...	1	—	
Saddles, I.A. luggage, large	1	—	
Straps, girth	4	—	
Harness, double shaft, farmers draught:—			
Bands, back, short	1	—	
Bands, belly	1	—	
Saddlery, universal:—			
‡Bits, portmouth, reversible, large ...	2	2	‡ Or "bits, snaffle, van," to any percentage found desirable.
Heads, bridle, extra large	2	2	
Blankets, saddle	1	1	
Collars, head, extra large	2	2	
Girths, leather, pattern '84	1	1	
Leathers, stirrup	2	2	
Pannels, numnah ... ... pairs	1	1	
§Reins, bit	2	2	
Saddles, S.A.	1	1	§ " Reins, bearing," for " off " horses can be used in lieu.
Stirrups	2	2	
Straps, baggage	6	3	
Surcingles, leather	2	1	

The following extending straps should be demanded where necessary for fitting harness to heavy draught horses:—

Breechings, straps, extending ...	For extending breechings one is used at each end of breeching; also for extending neck-piece pole-bar, one or more as necessary.
Surcingles, straps, extending ...	For extending surcingle; neck straps and straps, hip, long, wheel, as necessary.
Girths, pieces, extending ...	For extending girths.

ND - #0533 - 270225 - C0 - 195/125/2 - PB - 9781908487728 - Matt Lamination